AF876669

more favorite CLASSICS

SOLO BOOK TWO

19 Favorite Pieces for Late Intermediate through Early Advanced Students from the Four Stylistic Periods of Piano Repertoire

Selected & Edited by E. L. Lancaster & Kenon D. Renfrow

About This Collection

The 19 pieces in this collection have proven to be favorites of late intermediate through early advanced students throughout the years. Chosen from the four stylistic periods of piano repertoire, the volume contains selections of varying difficulty levels so that it may be used over a two- to three-year period.

A companion volume, *More Favorite Classics—Accompaniment Book Two* (#32083), contains specially composed second keyboard parts for a teacher, parent or more advanced student. The second keyboard part may be played on a second piano or electronic instrument and may be recorded or sequenced to enhance practice, learning and performance. The pieces in each collection have a page-by-page cross reference, and measures are numbered for ease of use.

Alfred Music Publishing Co., Inc.
P.O. Box 10003
Van Nuys, CA 91410-0003
alfred.com

ISBN-10: 0-7390-5873-8
ISBN-13: 978-0-7390-5873-2

Suggested Order of Study

The following is a suggested order of study for late intermediate through early advanced levels. Students should study pieces from two or more style periods simultaneously.

Late Intermediate

Early Advanced

Contents

Use with
MORE FAVORITE CLASSICS
Accompaniment Book Two,
page 3.

Prelude in G Major

George Frideric Handel
(1685–1759)

13
mf
f
dim.
16
mp
19
cresc.
22
f
dim.
25
2nd time rit.
1.
2.

Use with
MORE FAVORITE CLASSICS
Accompaniment Book Two,
page 6.

Invention No. 14 in B-flat Major

Johann Sebastian Bach (1685–1750)
BWV 785

* Play the eighth notes slightly detached throughout unless marked otherwise.

11
mf
p
cresc.
13
f
dim.
p
15
f
p
mf
p
mp
p
mf
17
cresc.
19
f

Use with
MORE FAVORITE CLASSICS
Accompaniment Book Two,
page 10.

Gavotte

(French Suite No. 5 in G Major)

Johann Sebastian Bach (1685–1750)
BWV 816

* Play the quarter notes slightly detached throughout unless marked otherwise.

13
cresc.
mf
16
mp
19
cresc.
mf
22
dim.
mp

Use with
MORE FAVORITE CLASSICS
Accompaniment Book Two,
page 12.

Little Prelude in C Major

Johann Sebastian Bach (1685–1750)
BWV 939

Use with
MORE FAVORITE CLASSICS
Accompaniment Book Two,
page 14.

Für Elise

Ludwig van Beethoven (1770–1827)
WoO 59

21
1.
2.
25
mp
29
p
33
36
dim.
pp

41
45
49
53
57
p

62
f
dim.
67
p
72
f
77
p
pp
poco cresc.
81
8va
pp

85
89
mf
93
dim.
97
101
dim.
poco rit.

Use with
MORE FAVORITE CLASSICS
Accompaniment Book Two,
page 20.

Sonatina in G Major

Ludwig van Beethoven
(1770–1827)

17
p
21
25
mf
28
31

Use with MORE FAVORITE CLASSICS
Accompaniment Book Two, page 23.

ROMANZE

Allegretto

20
mf
24
28
p
32
mp
36
p

Use with
MORE FAVORITE CLASSICS
Accompaniment Book Two,
page 26.

Sonatina in C Major

Friedrich Kuhlau (1786–1832)
Op. 55, No. 3

sem

legato
mf
cresc.
f
p
cresc.

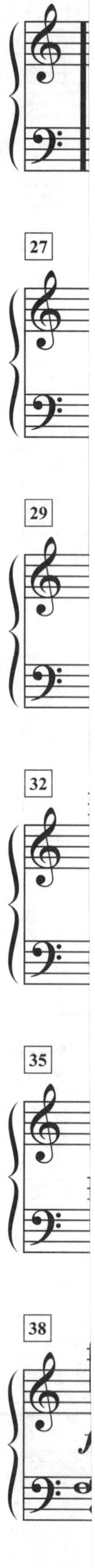

Use with MORE FAVORITE CLASSICS
Accompaniment Book Two,
page 31.

Use with
MORE FAVORITE CLASSICS
Accompaniment Book Two,
page 56.

Waltz in A Minor

Frédéric François Chopin (1810–1849)
Op. Posthumous

* Play the grace notes on the beat.

17
mf
21
25
p
29
33
f
mf

55
f
58
mp
legato
p
61
mf
64
67
70

Use with
MORE FAVORITE CLASSICS
Accompaniment Book Two,
page 45.

Witches' Dance

Theodor Kullak (1818–1882)
Op. 4, No. 2

26
ff
p
32
a tempo
poco rit.
pp
38
p
44
mf
p
50
sfz
sfz
dim.
pp

Use with
MORE FAVORITE CLASSICS
Accompaniment Book Two,
page 48.

About Strange Lands and People

(Scenes from Childhood)

Robert Schumann (1810–1856)
Op. 15, No. 1

Andante con moto

10
rit.
13
a tempo
p
16
19
2nd time poco rit.

Use with
MORE FAVORITE CLASSICS
Accompaniment Book Two,
page 50.

Prelude in E Minor

Frédéric François Chopin (1810–1849)
Op. 28, No. 4

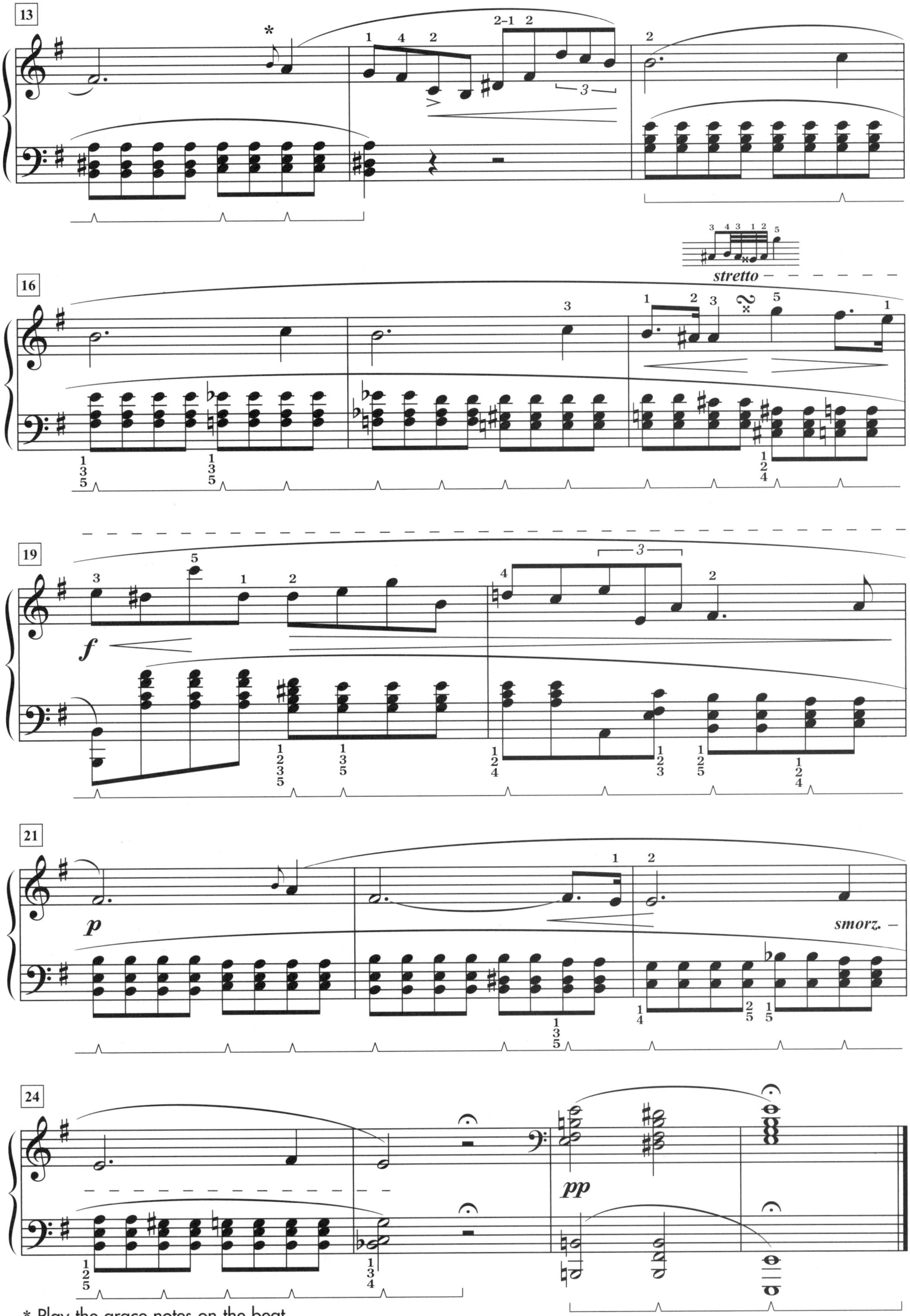

* Play the grace notes on the beat.

Use with
MORE FAVORITE CLASSICS
Accompaniment Book Two,
page 52.

Prelude in C Minor

Frédéric François Chopin (1810–1849)
Op. 28, No. 20

37
f
41
p
45
p
49
53
tr

Use with MORE FAVORITE CLASSICS Accompaniment Book Two, page 60.

Fluttering Leaves

Carl Kölling (1831–1914)
Op. 147, No. 2

22
f
fz
fz
mp
27
p
31
35
pp
40

45
50
dim.
55
a tempo
poco rall.
59
f
fz
mp

63
poco a poco a tempo
f
fz
poco rall.
fz
mp
67
71
cresc.
75
ff
p

Use with
MORE FAVORITE CLASSICS
Accompaniment Book Two,
page 66.

Venetian Boat Song

(Songs without Words)

Felix Mendelssohn (1809–1847)
Op. 19, No. 6

24
p
28
sfz
32
dim.
p
mf
37
pp
RH
42

Use with
MORE FAVORITE CLASSICS
Accompaniment Book Two,
page 70.

Bagatelle

Alexander Tcherepnin (1899–1977)
Op. 5, No. 1

9
p
11
13
15
8va
8va

Use with
MORE FAVORITE CLASSICS
Accompaniment Book Two,
page 73.

A Giddy Girl

(Histoires)

Jacques Ibert
(1890–1962)

15
cédez et diminuez (slow down and diminish)
LH
en exagérant les nuances
(exaggerating the dynamics)
18
au mouvt
pp
poco
21
un peu retenu
LH
au mouvt
24
cresc.
LH
f
27

Use with
MORE FAVORITE CLASSICS
Accompaniment Book Two,
page 76.

The Little White Donkey

(Histoires)

Jacques Ibert
(1890–1962)

13
16
19
soutenu (sustained)
22
mf
26
un peu cédé (a little ritard.)

Soudain très gai
(suddenly very lively)

42
45
en exagérant un peu les accents
(exaggerate the accents a little)
48
diminuez
(diminishing)
51
Un peu ralenti
(a little slower)
long

Avec la même humeur paisible du début
(with the same peaceful mood as at the beginning)
54
très léger
ppp
57
60
63
66

69
72
75
poco
78
retenez un peu (ritard. a little)
81
au mouvt (a tempo)
pp
poco sf
8va

Use with
MORE FAVORITE CLASSICS
Accompaniment Book Two,
page 84.

Golliwogg's Cakewalk

(Children's Corner Suite)

Claude Debussy
(1862–1918)

26
31
più p
36
41
più p
47
Un peu moins vite
(a little slower)

53
pp
<pp>
58
Cédez, avec une grande émotion
(slower, with great emotion)
p
63
a tempo
p
pp
Cédez
a tempo
p
pp
68
Cédez
mf
f
a tempo
73
Cédez
p
a tempo
pp
Cédez
p

78
a tempo
83
dim.
retenez (holding back)
più p
88
toujours retenu (always holding back)
92
Tempo I
97
molto

102
108
113
118
124